MW00807111

What is Stoicism?

2021 Edition

© Copyright 2021- All rights reserved.

The content contained within this book may not be reproduced, duplicated or transmitted without direct written permission from the author or the publisher.

Under no circumstances will any blame or legal responsibility be held against the publisher, or author, for any damages, reparation, or monetary loss due to the information contained within this book. Either directly or indirectly.

Legal Notice: This book is copyright protected. This book is only for personal use. You cannot amend, distribute, sell, use, quote or paraphrase any part, or the content within this book, without the consent of the author or publisher.

Disclaimer Notice: Please note the information contained within this document is for educational and entertainment purposes only. All effort has been executed to present accurate, up to date, and reliable, complete information. No warranties of any kind are declared or implied. Readers acknowledge that the author is not engaging in the rendering of legal, financial, medical or professional advice. The content within this book has been derived from various sources. Please consult a licensed professional before attempting any techniques outlined in this book.

By reading this document, the reader agrees that under no circumstances is the author responsible for any losses, direct or indirect, which are incurred as a result of the use of information contained within this document, including, but not limited to, — errors, omissions, or inaccuracies.

Contents

Introduction

Stoicism. It is a philosophy designed to make us stronger, happier, more virtuous, and wiser, and as a result, better people, better parents, and better professionals.

Stoicism is the famous ancient Greek philosophy founded by Zeno of Citium in Athens, while it was precariously in the 3rd century BC. C. To be stoic is to be in the eye of a hurricane and be still and calm amidst whirlwinds of chaos and destruction. It merely is not a philosophy but a way of life that transforms the lives of many.

A philosophy that was created many years ago, stoicism is still incredibly useful, even in the modern era. Stoic philosophy was derived from controlling emotions. A stoic person does not complain and can easily face difficulties. Undoubtedly, stoicism can also help endure pain.

Becoming stoic can be difficult, but through this technique, you can master your thoughts. As the name of this book suggests, you can learn and master stoicism quite effectively.

How does he become stoic? Well, this book is the answer to that question. This philosophy can make you more reliable, and emotional confusion won't affect you if you learn to behave like a stoic.

The chapters in this book are full of history, philosophy, and practical exercises to better understand stoicism. I hope this book is helpful and changes your mindset significantly. I wish you all the best on the journey that begins now!

What is Stoicism?

There are some morals of stoicism, such as prudence, strength, justice, and moderation.

How often do you worry about your thoughts? That continuous tommyrot of trash running in your mind? These unnecessary thoughts of worry and negativity could be the reason for your pain or grief. This is the good news: You can take control of your thinking through the surprising and practically methodical philosophy of stoicism.

Many great people have practiced it, one of whom was the Roman king Marcus Aurelius. The Emperor was a paradoxical example of stoicism. Another famous historical person was Epictetus, and beyond him, there are many more examples.

Chapter 1

What does stoicism do to humanity?

Stoicism empowers us over our thought process and enables us to be resilient enough to face life's difficulties. It can also save a soul from chaos. It is merely about resistance (mental, not necessarily physical) and our ability to be patient and to control negative emotions. Many other things happen to a stoic person, such as a renewed admiration for reality, a greater sense of justice, belief in themselves, and a better attitude towards life in general. Put merely, stoicism illuminates the mind and promotes a better experience by taking self-control over destructive thoughts. It is the art of balancing human feelings and emotions.

You can master your thoughts and improve your energy. Don't you find it incredibly enriching to get to know yourself better, control your thoughts in a way that benefits you, and find harmony in life? Stoicism encompasses acceptance, and if the outcome of any situation is good or bad, it keeps you calm. It teaches you to accept reality.

According to science, the human mind is full of memories. But where does this memory come from? I would say experience more than thoughts. There may be individual experiences that create specific ideas. For example, childhood trauma can never be forgotten. This trauma can give your designs an eternal impression.

Thoughts are the foundations of human nature. You are what you think. Perception makes a big difference.

According to the great Marco Aurelio, "It takes very little to make a happy life; everything is within you, in your way of thinking" (Marco Aurelio, Hard, Marco Aurelio, and Fronto, 2011).
We will understand this deeply. Thoughts are seeds that grow within us.
When you can grow a rose (right thinking), then why should you grow marijuana (lousy thought)? Every day and every second of your life, you are doing some kind of action. They can be physical, mental, or emotional. In their entirety, these actions are closely related to feelings, or we could say emotions. These thoughts create feelings, and beliefs create emotions. Emotions, in turn, produce chemicals in our body and mind. In natural language, you can call them "hormones."

Thoughts, feelings, emotions, and hormones give rise to some kind of energy within the body. It could be positive energy or negative energy. Stoicism quenches negative thoughts and negative behaviors. Promote a positive attitude towards life. It allows you to see reality as it is and also helps you with acceptance. Ultimately, stoicism changes the mindset.

Epictetus was a stoic philosopher from the 1st century AD, and together with Marcus Aurelius and Seneca, he is known to be one of the significant Stoic philosophers' figures. If you read more about him, you will discover that his teachings are fascinating.

Epictetus spent a part of his life as a slave in the city of Hierapolis in Asia Minor. The fact that Epictetus was once a slave gives credibility and authority to his teachings. As you know, stoicism is mostly about living as content with life as possible, regardless of the circumstances. I can't help but feel that Epictetus's experience as a slave would have taught him a lot about acceptance and satisfaction. That shines through in his words.

He has written some of the best quotes and specific ideas for Stoic teachers that I think are relevant to us and also representative of stoicism in general. He said that everyone has to die, and he must too. He explained his slavery by saying that his body was chained, but not his mind. Also, he added that no one could take his smile away. I think these ideas are an excellent introduction to the central Stoic concept: the idea that we finally control our impressions and feelings. According to the Stoics, our will is our most precious possession as human beings.

Our will is our ability to make sound and reasonable judgments about our circumstances, and although our bodies may suffer or be imprisoned, they will never have to submit. Therefore, we can remain content even in the most challenging circumstances. The only wives that could catch our minds are our thoughts. Similarly, our brains have the power to undo all the handcuffs that can be thrown at us. We should all be familiar with the idea of gaining satisfaction through the use of our will.

It is also worth considering how Stoics views the world. The world can be divided into two broad categories, and this is a straightforward equation. Some things are out of our control, that is, all externalities and all circumstances outside of ourselves, and then some things are under our control, and all can be reduced to our will. The will is of vital importance since we can use it to prevent these externalities from interrupting our internal sense of satisfaction or equanimity. There are many quotes from Marcus, where he refers to luck and will. His words are so powerfully represented that he used fortune instead of circumstance and faculty instead of a will. Thus,

The question is, why should we let circumstances override our will? The answer is to be happy. Now let's go back to the word equanimity. It is often associated with stoicism and is generally taken to mean composure, impartiality, or impassivity. But there are more sources than the simple acceptance of stone. Patience is also full of gratitude. Appreciation for the fact that we are inhabiting this universe or on the scale of the greatness of this universe. Therefore, it is not correct to dismiss this philosophy only by tolerating bad things. Stoicism is an even theistic philosophy, which means that all items are parts of a sacred whole. There is another quote that illustrates that idea very well. That quote says that each human is connected to another. Man is also united with God,

But even so, we cannot forget that stoicism is closely related to obligations. It is not enough for us to live a life of absolute pleasure. The condition that we have desire requires that we are exposed to all the pain that the universe could throw at us. We need to accept everything as part of the whole. We cannot choose what life throws at us. Everything is delivered in a constant stream of totality. This requires that we have a broader perspective of our circumstances than we might be used to having. Epictetus gives us a great example when he asks us to consider that we have broken our legs, and we appreciate that this is much better than living without legs.

Since we are part of this tremendous incredible universe, we must accept what happens to us for the good of all. To return to that topic of joy and gratitude, another concept is my favorite lesson. It reminds me that when I'm alone, I don't need to consider it a miserable and isolated condition. I don't need to feel like I'm missing out. Instead, I can see it as an opportunity to reflect on tranquility.
Similarly, when I am in a crowd, there is no reason to withdraw. Instead, I should take the opportunity to network with my human companions to form connections and interact. This is encouraging stoic advice.

Famous followers of stoicism

JK Rowling

The immensely successful best-selling author of the Harry Potter franchise is a follower of Stoic philosophy. She is a continuous follower of Marco Aurelio, and he is one of her favorite philosophers. Their appointments and meditations helped Rowling a lot in his awkward moments. Keep in mind that before JK Rowling was a billionaire and a household name, she was just like anyone else. She went through 38 different rejections while caring for her family as a single mother. Therefore, he went through a fair amount of adversity and used the stoic mindset of turning obstacles into means to move forward. When many other people would have stopped and abandoned, she would continue. She is a follower of philosophy.

Neil Strauss

Author of The Game, Neil Strauss listed Seneca's On the Shortness of Life as one of his favorite books. The exciting thing about this essay by Seneca is that it deals with the fact that we, as humans, think that life is short, when, in fact, our life is not short. We have plenty of time to do what we want. It's just that we waste a lot of time on minor matters. We think about our neighbors; we spend time on things that are not going to comply or items that are not going to matter in the future. Neil Strauss's story is fascinating because he was selected as a writer for the New York Times magazine. After a time, he became a collecting artist. He was later kicked out of the magazine. He got over it and became a bestselling author.

Lupe Fiasco

Award-winning Grammy-conscious rap artist Lupe Fiasco is known to be an avid reader of the principles of stoicism. In one of his songs "Lightwork," he dropped the following line; "The Emperor is his alias, but not Marco Aurelio. Lupe Fiasco is known for recommending Marcus Aurelio's meditations. He has adapted many quotes and reflections from Marco Aurelio in his life. Not only that, he even recommends reading and following Stoicism and Marco Aurelio's teachings to everyone. He suggests that everyone absorb the stoic wisdom presented by the Emperor himself, Marco Aurelio, so that we can all communicate on the same level and live a better life.

Nassim Nicholas Taleb

Another famous Stoic is Nassim Nicholas Taleb, who is a Lebanese American essayist, academic esthetician, as well as a former trader and risk analysis. He is known for his best-selling book, Anti Fragile, where he talks about the antifragility of Stoic philosophy, especially Seneca's philosophy. According to him, a stoic is someone who can transform their insecurities or fears into prudence, pain in transformation, errors in the initiation, and wishes or wishes in the company. He summed up the practicalities of stoicism. Stoicism has the power to turn every negative aspect of your life into something positive, as well as to turn every situation into a way to grow and improve. Stoicism is based on perception. It's all about attitude. So, We can determine the quality of our life by how we choose to perceive the events that happen. This is how famous philosophers have explained what our life should be like. So a stoic is someone who sees the negative and chooses to transform it into good or something that can help them.

Bill Clinton

The most famous person on this list is the former President of the United States, Bill Clinton. He was a great admirer of Marco Aurelio and his meditations. He said that he read the book once a year while President, which would make sense because Marco Aurelio's reflections were like a personal diary for the Emperor in which he wrote notes on how he could live. Better, become nobler, and live a virtuous life by nature. Bill Clinton would have received a lot of courage reading these notes, especially since people don't change. Technology changes, but the human condition has not improved. We still face the same adversities in leadership and life. Bill Clinton said that the thing about Marcus Aurelius is that he was profoundly spiritual and understood that life requires balance. His books also show what not to do as Emperor. He has mentioned what he would not do, and that is important. Marco Aurelio heavily influenced Bill Clinton.

These are all personalities who wholeheartedly believe in living their lives to the fullest and not being caught in any traditional role that is part of it. One second is almost a fraction of our lives, and yet our lives are long enough as long as we can imagine. We need to make sure that we live our lives to the fullest.

Chapter 2: History of stoicism-philosophers and their vision.

Stoicism was founded by Zeno of Citium, of Phoenician descent. Unfortunately, there are only piecemeal Zeno quotes available today.
Stoicism first appeared in Athens in the Hellenistic period around 301 BC. C. Zeno taught at the Stoa Poikile (the painted porch). This is where stoicism got its name. Very little is known about Zeno's writings, and what we have gathered has been reconstructed by his students and followers.
Zeno was followed by Cleanthes, then Chrysippus, and even later by Panaetius and Posidonius. Only three ancient Stoics, Seneca, Epictetus, and Marcus Aurelius, survive incomplete books. None of the first three philosophers had a broad audience. Very little is available from any of these philosophers, except in second-hand accounts (Sharpe, 2013).
Stoicism underwent an evolution from "living according to" to "living according to nature" to "living according to the experience of what happens by nature." Stoicism is very versatile because it is applied continuously to what matters today. Although all these philosophers had their differences and helped lay the foundations of patience, what we know to be true today will continue to be different from what they believed then.
We will go more into the three foremost philosophers, as well as other notable figures, in the last part of the chapter. First, before we get too stoic, we have to understand what the point of everything was.

Stoic Happiness Triangle
Stoicism is about being okay with what happens "by nature," even in confusing and / or uncertain times. Many people think that the secret to being happy is to rid your life of anything terrible. This is the reason why so many people will spend their entire lives unhappy.
The Stoics' goal is to live according to nature, and from there, they will become virtuous. It is not that they will be happy once they are upright, but that they find happiness. Instead of waiting in misery to be satisfied, Stoics knows how to turn that misery into something productive. From that change, positivity arises, and the prospects change for the better.

Eudaimonia
At the center of the triangle is eudaimonia, the end goal of life agreed in all ancient philosophies. Eudaimonia is a word that has been translated to have different meanings, but deep down, there are some things that this phrase has in common between interpretations.

Eudaimonia is what we can get out of bad times to be happy. It is a state in which we are satisfied, content, and comfortable. We understand how to be happy, and small things are not that annoying. Eudaimonia has many interpretations and is discussed frequently because it will always look different in each individual, no matter what they believe in (Baltzly, 2008).

Live with earring

Express your highest self in every moment. To be happy, we must continuously be doing our best. We should use excellence in everything we do, and we should never settle for anything less. Living with an earring means that we know what it is to have virtue, and we no longer allow ourselves to live without it. Many Stoics believe that this means that a person is living to her full potential.

This is something that can be difficult to do, but it is a challenge that Stoics accept and will pursue on their journey to the good life.

Focus on what you control

Focus on the things we control and rest as it happens. A stoic is continually looking at the difference between something that is in and out of his control. The reason so many people will struggle to find real happiness in their lives is that they are trying too hard to take control where it does not belong to them.

This is also going to be a challenge, but something else the Stoics will try to do often. As we take you through the rest of this book, remember these three essential ideas. They are what constitutes the triangle of what the Stoics seek in the first place.

Zeno

Died: C. 262 BC; Athens, Greece (several decades after stoicism was founded)

Born: C. 334 a. Citium (Cyprus era: ancient philosophy)

Zeno founded stoicism as a commentary on the philosophical education of the time. Rather than forcing classmates to sit behind a desk for hours, he chose to take his teaching to a public space, where he could say controversial things out loud for people to talk about.

Zeno believed that happiness is "a good flow of life" or "living according." He was a rich man who lost a lot in a shipwreck. From there, he decided to enter a bookstore and became interested in philosophy. Stoicism arose in Zeno because he could not accept many of the cynical philosophies that he had already read. (Encyclopedia of Britannica, 2019)

Main interests

The logic was essential to Zeno. He often emphasized making sure that his wise followers were not victims of deception. Zeno was aware of the perceptions we created and felt that it was important to him to make others realize that they could alter this way of thinking.

Physics meant a lot to Zeno because he saw the universe as God Himself. Everything lived harmoniously together, and all the inner workings created a thing on which we all depended. He felt that there was a divine fire, much like energy that drives all the activity that exists in the universe.

Ethics was his last trinity of knowledge, and he felt that there was only one good. Anything that caused happiness had to be achieved through reason, a universal logo that governs everything. Anything that we consider to be bad would be pathos, and this is an alteration in the natural flow of things.

Cleanthes
Died: C. 230 a. Athens, Greece
Born: C. 330 BC; Assos School: Stoicism
Cleanthes became the leader of the Stoic school after Zeno's suicide.

Initially, he was a boxer who found an interest in philosophy, listening to Zeno's teacher Crates the Cynic, and then finally to Zeno himself. He was a very patient person, and for this reason, some people even gave him a slow reputation. Some eventually gave him the nickname "the donkey," to which he responded well. He noted this, meaning that his back was strong, in fact, durable enough to handle what Zeno asked of him (Ellery, 1976).

Main interests
Cleanthes knew that in the end, the most important thing was "living according to nature." I would argue that even our bodies, in the sense that they are separate from our minds, could be material possessions. If we were in mental agony, that could show up in our bodies, which is how the two are connected.

He was somewhat opposed to Zeno, as he believed that the divine fire that helped sustain all life was not the earth itself, but the sun that gives us so much power. Cleanthes also felt that any pleasure we experienced was not a good thing. He thought it was against nature and even "worthless." This is not true for all Stoics, and we will delve into this meaning throughout the book.

Chrysippus
Born: 279 BC, Soli, Cilicia (over a century after stoicism was founded)

Died: 206 BC, Athens, Greece

Chrysippus was another student at Cleanthes. It became part of the school after Zeno had passed, but it was still instilled with many of the same virtues. Chrysippus is said to have written 705 books. Through his writings, he was able to expand on what Zeno was taught, and eventually became known as the second founder of stoicism.

An interesting fact about Chrysippus is that he died of laughter. This is only proof that Stoics don't have to be emotionless.

Main interests

Chrysippus was primarily interested in protecting stoicism. He helped broaden the ideas, but he wrote them down and shared them in a way that was protected not only from the past but also from the future of stoicism.

He was known for his passion for education, and many thought it was even strange how much he enjoyed learning. He ended up becoming the school's principal also after Cleanthes died.

Other notable stoic influencers

The three scholars we have just discussed were undoubtedly crucial to the base of stoicism. However, we cannot overlook the others who eventually followed, who also helped shape it. Throughout the rest of the book, we won't go into history as much and instead focus on the philosophy these great scholars shared.

There will be quotes from some of the original Stoics as well, but the intention of the book is not to separate the story and take what applies to life now so that we can find some of the greatness these individuals did.

If we stick too closely to his exact words, we will not be able to find our path of happiness. We should emphasize what is the meaning behind what they said, rather than logistically separating it.

Panaetius of Rhodes

He was the seventh stoic school leader to appear after Zeno had already died. He helped create a branch of stoicism that was a little more eclectic.

Panaetius made changes to Stoic doctrines, emphasizing personal duty, and dismissing the need for a philosophical commitment to understand and achieve the Good Life. Rather than sticking to the strict ideas other Stoics had, he sought to make it more applicable to an individual's life, so that they could take stoicism and use it practically.

Posidonium of Apamea

He was a Stoic philosopher, astronomer, and geographer. Despite his abilities, he still felt that philosophy was an essential part of all. Even his most scientific works were still things based on philosophy. He firmly believed that our passions were connected to our human nature. It was not our fault for these passions, but rather, the ethics that we thought, that was the problem of how we react to these intrinsic passions.

Lucius Annaeus Seneca

He was also known as Seneca, the youngest, or most commonly, simply Seneca was a statesman, a philosopher, and a playwright. His father was Seneca the Elder, who was a prolific writer. He was exiled at one point in his life, only to return and be a mentor to the future Emperor Nero.

In 54 AD, when Nero finally became Emperor, he became his adviser. He helped create a competent world but eventually began to lose influence over Nero. He ultimately committed suicide after being accused of trying to assassinate Nero. He was also noted for having a reasonably quiet suicide, often depicted in paintings.

He is best known for his writings, which often quote and extract things from other great Stoics as well. He was incredibly tight in his ability to withstand certain elements, and will always be one of the most quoted Stoics.

Musonius Rufus

He was a stoic teacher and writer. He was the teacher of the next philosopher on the list, Epictetus. He was a great teacher, until Seneca's death, in which Musonio was also exiled. He still taught, but could no longer do so in stoicism's actual birthplace, and instead did so in exile, far from Athens. Eventually, he returned to Rome, only to be banished once again by all philosophers.

He was best known for discussing how Stoics could overcome everything evil, including death. It was not that death was inevitable; rather, Stoic principles could help us begin to fear this idea much less.

Hierapolis Epictetus

He was a philosopher and a student of Musonius Rufus. He is known for embracing life and all its challenges because he knew we had to do our best with what we could. For everything else, it was better if we could take it as it happens. The most surprising thing about him is not his origin story, but the fact that he never wrote anything! It was his students who monitored the knowledge he had to give to others.

Originally a slave, his name means "acquired." That is what separates stoicism from many other philosophies and even sciences of the time. Anyone was stoic, even Epictetus, who had been born a slave. His real name is something that is still unknown.

Marco Aurelio
He was the Roman Emperor from 161-180 AD. C. Marco Aurelio was the last great Emperor of ancient Rome and had a great passion for stoicism. Power was not something he sought, but something that had fallen into his possession. He was a great stoic leader because he was humble and fair. Although he could have whatever he wanted as a man with such power, he never lived beyond his means and knew there was no point in being overly excessive, an essential idea that we will discuss later.

Chapter 3: Modern Stoicism and General Misconceptions about Stoicism

Why are more and more people expressing interest in stoicism, to the point that there is an annual event dedicated to learning how to practice its principles in daily life? The short answer is that life is difficult, and any philosophy that teaches us how to deal with it is welcome.

Note that stoicism arose at a time when there was great turmoil in the world. People were no longer sure of their place in the world, and the certainty of the polis gave way to corrupt and inefficient rulers. Compare the conditions with what is happening in the world today, and it should come as no surprise why more people turn to stoicism to help them deal with unpredictable times. As Seneca points out, what you need to escape the things that harass you is not to be somewhere else but to be someone else.

Stoicism encourages us to see things as they are so that we can honestly learn how to solve our problems, even if it is only in the way we perceive them. Therefore, stoicism is opposed to self-help philosophies such as those based on "The Secret," which encourages us not to commit to reality but to visualize our wishes in the hope that they will come true.

However, stoicism does not advocate a retreat in our world, but a commitment to the external world and other human beings. According to the ancient Stoics, practicing virtue meant serving other people and encouraging a cosmopolitan in which people saw themselves as citizens of the world that were not defined by class, religion, or country.

Stoics used the concept of ketosis to define our relationships with others. The term comes from the Greek word for home or family and means seeing something that belongs to you. In other words, as Stoics, we should extend our affinities not only to our families but also to our fellow citizens and, moving away, to all peoples. As Marco Aurelio said, what happens to you is good for the world, but what happens to a single individual is also for the good of others.

Therefore, as Stoics, we seek not only our good but also that of others. This is particularly important in a globalized world where people have to work together to solve some of the most pressing problems. Addressing climate change, for example, means that nations must embrace global agreements and treaties.

Agnostics and Atheists

Another answer is that stoicism provides an alternative belief system to traditional organized religion. Unlike religion, which is based on dogma and revealed knowledge, stoicism thrives on free inquiry and reason. We must use our goal to guide us to the truth and understand the nature of reality.

The Stoics' insistence on reason as the governing law of the universe can be very liberating for formerly religious people who have tried to live their lives based on the strict and often illogical religions such as Christianity or Islam. This stoic principle may have penetrated the public consciousness, which explains the common phrase, "everything happens for a reason."

At the same time, there is room for doubt and uncertainty in stoicism. You don't need to have all the answers; the important thing is that you train yourself to reason so that you can do the right thing,

But stoicism can also be welcoming to Christians due to stoic belief in a God who created the universe and directs it with a purpose. Of course, not all Stoics appreciated God the same way: some worshiped him, like Cleanthes of Assos, who wrote a "Hymn to Zeus," while others seem to have been more agnostic. Panaetius, the last head of the Athenian Stoic school, reportedly said that arguing about the gods has negligible value for the Stoic way of life.

The primary reason for this ambiguity is that the Stoics do not perceive God (Zeus, as the ancient Stoics referred to him) in traditional religious terms, but as the personification of nature. Zenón, the founder of

Stoicism was said to have been inspired to become a philosopher in "The Choice of Hercules," a symbolic work by Prodicus. Prodicus reinterpreted the ancient gods as personifications of natural phenomena such as the moon, sun, and rivers, and this led to accusations of atheism. The philosopher Cicero accused Perseus, one of Zeno's most prominent immediate students, of being an atheist, since he also interpreted the gods in the same way.

Ultimately, however, stoicism is a philosophy that embraces both religious and agnostics. The fundamental human virtue is wisdom, and it is not necessary to believe in God to accept this.

Promoting gratitude

One of the biggest misconceptions about stoicism is that it's just about enduring life's hardships. But Stoics also promotes the idea that we should enjoy life, no matter what it brings. As Seneca said, the happy man is content with his lot in life, whatever it is, and reconciles with his current circumstances.

To promote their sense of gratitude, the ancient Stoics used techniques such as engaging with "outsiders" such as fame, money, or even good health, to remind themselves that the only important thing is a virtue. They would also undergo voluntary discomfort, such as giving up something they craved or taking cold showers, to foster a greater appreciation of food or heat, for example.

This principle of stoicism is becoming very popular in today's self-help movement, where people are encouraged to thank their loved ones for what they have done and to keep diaries of gratitude where they write things for which they are grateful. To achieve recognition, self-help gurus also encourage followers to practice mindfulness through focused exercises and to be fully present in the moment.

For the ancient Stoics, practicing mindfulness was very important, as it allowed them to be more self-aware and therefore, to have more control of their emotions and to be able to separate and see things in a broader context. As the philosopher Epictetus said, men, are not bothered by circumstances, but by their views. So, he advised, don't expect things to go your way, but expect them to happen as they will, and you will get along.

There was also a technique that the ancients practiced called premeditation Malorum, where they would visualize the worst that could happen in any situation. This would allow them to prepare to face it mentally or, as Seneca said, to minimize our fear of life's misfortunes and be ready to meet them.

Preparing for the worst can be seen as a refutation of The Secret and similar positive-thinking self-help philosophies. By being ready for the worst that life has to bring, we can learn to be happy and develop a strong sense of gratitude for the many good things that life brings us.

Because there is so much information in this chapter, I will take a moment to recap some of the most critical factors. First, you must remember that stoicism is not intended to teach you how to be insensitive. You are still going to have your emotions, and you are always going to feel these emotions. Stoicism does not want to take away your feelings. Patience is here to help you better manage your feelings so that you can make rational decisions instead of emotional decisions.

Stoicism wants to help you learn how to process your emotions before making a decision. If you don't learn to process your feelings, you will make an irrational decision, which can harm you and those around you in various ways. For example, if you are excited, you may feel that you can achieve more than you really can. When you realize that you can't handle what you said to yourself and others you can handle, you start to feel like a failure. But, this does not make you a failure; it makes you a person who overestimated what they could do due to emotions. Remember, stoicism also teaches us to learn from our mistakes. If you are in this position, you can learn from the error so you can better estimate your task.

It is essential to remove your emotions from any decision you make because other emotions may appear when you realize that you are unable to complete the task on time. For example, you may start to feel anxious, stressed, and embarrassed. These emotions will not help you when you need to focus on a task. Stoicism wants to teach people how to focus on positive emotions and manage their negative emotions better so that they can achieve their purposes in life and be successful.

Stoicism focuses on giving you exercises and a mindset so that you can become the best person you can be, not so you can be better than anyone else. This is often a common mistake among people who do not understand stoicism. People who do not understand stoicism often feel that those who practice are trying to be better than others. But, all a stoic wants to do is focus on becoming the best person possible so that he can bring this good to the world and help others.

To truly and honestly help another person, you must understand how to improve the person. For example, if you want to help someone find happiness, make sure you are happy. If you're going to help someone find their self-esteem and get high self-esteem, you need to make sure you understand their self-worth and have the right amount of self-confidence. Stoics want to help themselves find their greatest happiness and self-esteem so they can focus on their purposes in life, but they also want to help others achieve their goals.

Stoicism is not a religion; It is a philosophy. Many people view patience as a religion because many of the early Stoics spoke of the Greek gods in their writings. However, stoicism is intended to be a philosophy. Think of it this way: Religions tend to care about how you act in this world because you want to get to Heaven. While this is an excellent way of thinking, it is not the purpose of stoicism.

Stoicism wants people to achieve their highest good so that they can live the best life on earth. Patience is not focused on reaching future growth; it focuses on what you can do to make the world a better place for yourself and others. Of course, Stoics have nothing against any religion, and most Stoics follow their chosen religion. But, it is essential to remember that it is not a religion. It is a philosophy to help you learn the best way of life you can live.

Chapter 4: Basic Concepts of Stoicism

The basic principle of stoicism is that some things are under your control, and others are not. According to great Stoic philosophers like Epictetus and Marcus Aurelius, the leading cause of unhappiness is to confuse things that are not under his control for items that are. When you look for happiness in something that you cannot control, you suffer anxiety and stress.
When you seek happiness only in things that you control, you are free.

If this seems like a simple idea, it is because it is. You don't have to understand any abstract metaphysical concepts to understand stoicism. All you have to do is accept and try to live according to this simple idea. It is not worth worrying about what is not under your control. Only things that are under your control should worry you at all.

Epictetus offers four examples of things that are not under your control: your body, your property, your reputation, and the amount of authority you have over others. These are just examples, but they cover many of the problems people face in life.

If there is one thing that most of us assume we have control of, it is our own body. Epictetus invites us to ask ourselves if this control is real or an illusion. Can you guarantee that you will never suffer from illness or injury? Can you prevent your body from aging? Nobody can. In the most extreme circumstances, you may no longer be able to move. Your body is something you don't control.

The same is true of your property. "A man's house is his castle," as people say, but he can lose that house to foreclosure or bankruptcy. Your car can be stolen. Your building can catch fire. As much as you want, you don't control your property.

Reputation is another example. No matter how hard you work to develop your business, anonymous social media reviews can significantly damage your reputation. The same is true for your private life. You can think of yourself as a right and honest person, but you cannot control what others think of you.

Authority, or "command," as Epictetus calls it, is also beyond his control. Your ability to command other people depends on your role in any organization you work for and your subordinates' willingness or capacity to do as you ask. If you are not in a position of authority, you cannot command others. Even if you are, you cannot be sure that they will choose to obey you. If they follow you, you cannot be sure that they will do a good job.

Think about how you would feel if you were seriously ill, if you lost your home in bankruptcy, if other people saw you as a wrong person, or if you could never make other people do what you wanted them to do. If you are like most people, you would be unhappy if any of these things happened, but you do not have the power to prevent them from happening.

Epictetus tells us that we cannot be free and that we can never be delighted, as long as our happiness depends on things that we cannot control. Because we cannot control our bodies, our property, our reputation, or our ability to command others, we must think of all these things as irrelevant to our happiness.

The power of choice

If we have no control over our bodies, our property, our reputation, or our ability to command others, what do we have control over? According to Epictetus:

"Things under our control are opinion, search, desire, aversion, and, in a word, whatever our actions are."

Human nature

Stoics considered nature to be the ultimate guide to human behavior, so why did they teach people to ignore perfectly natural emotions? To understand this particular aspect of Stoic philosophy, we must consider what kind of nature we share with all other creatures and what kind of life is exclusively human.

Hunger is something we share with all other living things. It could be said to be part of our shared animal nature. When a cat is hungry, it will always eat if it has food in its bowl. A hungry wolf will still hunt, and a hungry cow will always chew grass. A hungry person generally eats if given the opportunity, but there are situations where people choose not to eat.

For example, a person may choose not to eat because the only food available is unhealthy or because it is against a special diet they have chosen to follow. People sometimes fast for religious reasons or want not to eat to make a point, like on a hunger strike. While hunger is part of our shared animal nature, choosing whether or not to eat is exclusively human.

This faculty of choice, the Stoics called the "ruling faculty," is our human nature, which we do not share with other animals. A horse that did not act like a horse would seem unnatural to us. According to the Stoics, a human who does not exercise the governing faculty is equally false.

Because we have the natural ability to make rational decisions, we cannot fulfill our nature as human beings unless we make full use of that ability. While it may be natural for a dog to swallow all available food, even if it makes him feel ill later, it is more natural for a human to exercise restraint and avoid getting sick.

Virtue and happiness
The ability to make rational decisions is what the Stoics called "virtue," and they considered it the secret of happiness. The happiest life for a lion is to live like a lion, and the most comfortable experience for a human being is to live like a human being. Since the only thing that distinguishes us from other creatures is our ability to make rational decisions, the use of that ability is all we need to be truly happy. Therefore virtue and happiness are the same things for the Stoics.

There was considerable disagreement among the ancient Greek philosophers about the nature of happiness and the best way to achieve it. Almost all the old Greek schools of philosophy taught that no one could be happy without living a virtuous life, but they disagreed on how central virtue was too general happiness.

For Aristotle's followers, happiness was a combination of virtue and what we would think of as good fortune. If you were reasonably wealthy, healthy, handsome, and virtuous, they would say you are happy.

For followers of Epicurus, virtue was primarily a simple matter of increasing pleasure in his life while reducing pain. The main reason for being virtuous, according to the Epicureans, was to avoid all the stress and anxiety caused by making poor decisions.

The Stoics disagreed vehemently with both positions. If happiness depends on wealth, health, and good looks, then most people have little chance of being happy. Stoics were interested in finding a way of life that could bring happiness to anyone who practiced it, regardless of life circumstances. If satisfaction is just a matter of experiencing the greatest possible pleasure and least possible pain, virtue has little to do with it. The Stoics wanted people to be happy and enjoyable so that happiness was something much better than mere pleasure.

For the Stoics, the other schools of Greek philosophy were only looking for a kind of partial and dependent happiness, a happiness that could be lost as quickly as it was earned. They wanted more, but they also wanted it to be available to everyone.

That is why the Stoics taught a different and much more unusual doctrine: true happiness and virtue are the same things, allowing a person to be entirely happy regardless of the circumstances.

If you are happy, regardless of the circumstances, you do not need wealth or authority or a good reputation. You don't even need health, which most people consider a minimum for happiness. You have everything you need, and you can never lose it. As long as you exercise your governing power, everything else is indifferent.

Indifferent things

Most people would describe health, wealth, a positive reputation, and authority as "good," and most people would describe the opposites of all those things as "bad." According to Stoics, none of those things is good or bad because none can make you happy or unhappy. Nobody wants to be sick, but some sick people feel happy and healthy people who feel miserable. Nobody wants to be reduced, but some poor people feel so glad and rich people who feel unhappy.

If none of these things is good or bad, they can only be indifferent, and that's precisely what the Stoics called them. In Stoicism, everything that is not under your control is mentioned as nonchalant to emphasize that it is not essential to happiness.

It is still the case that no one would intentionally choose to be unhealthy or weak or to have a bad reputation. Although being rich is not good, it is perfectly natural to prefer wealth to poverty. Although being sick isn't bad, it's also natural to try to avoid illness.

In Stoic philosophy, it is okay to prefer some things to others, as long as you remember that they are still "indifferent," meaning that they are not essential to happiness for yourself or anyone else. Since they are not necessary, you can be happy if you have them or not.

Stoics consider essential for happiness the skillful and rational use of the governing faculty or, in a word, "virtue." Stoic virtue includes all traditional virtues, such as courage, temperance, justice, and wisdom, but defines them all as the simple use of rational choice.

For example, if you hear a child cry for help from inside a burning building, your first impression might be that the flames are terrifying, even though you would like to save them. A Stoic would have the same first impression. Still, it would rationally conclude that death is not unfortunate and that people must help and protect each other, whenever possible. This would lead the Stoics to act bravely and save the child.

Less dramatically, a Stoic might be as tempted as any other by a decadent buffet breakfast, but rationally he would choose to eat warmly and preserve his health. A stoic might be tempted to get angry at an irritating neighbor, but would act wisely and reasonably instead of instinct for anger.

In all cases, Stoics use our human power of choice (or "ruling power") to make rational and virtuous decisions rather than being carried away by emotional first impressions. Freed from fear and anxiety caused by false judgments, the Stoic is happy, no matter what.
Pathos
If Stoics are happy by definition, why do we use the word "Stoic" to describe people who don't seem to show any emotion? Not that the stoic is covering up all the painful feelings. That would not be happy at all. Instead, the Stoic is free from certain types of emotions that cause unnecessary suffering.

In modern English, the word "pathos" refers to a feeling of sadness or pity in a movie or book. If you feel sorry for one of the characters, that scene has pathos. The word "pathos" comes from the ancient Greek, and the Stoics used it to refer to the emotions that make people feel sorry for themselves.

For example, if your actions suddenly increased in value, you would probably be delighted. If the stock market collapsed, you would probably feel depressed and upset. The amount of your actions is not under your control, so your delight in one situation is the cause of your distress in the other case. For an ancient stoic thinker named Zeno of Citium, Delight and Distress are both pathê or types of pathos.

If you started dating someone you found very attractive, you would probably feel desire. If they stop returning your calls and text messages, you may feel scared. Whether someone wants to date you or not is under your control, so your desire in one situation causes fear. Hope and anxiety are also types of pathos.

In these pairs, a good emotion is combined with a seemingly lousy passion: delight with anguish and desire with fear.

"GOOD"	"BAD"
Delight	Anguish
Wish	Fear

These emotions can also be classified by when they occur in time. Delight refers to the present and desire for the future because hope is the anticipation of future happiness. Anxiety refers to the present and fear of the future because fear is the anticipation of future anguish.

PRESENT	FUTURE
Delight	Wish
Anguish	Fear

These four pathês or "passions" are all causes of suffering.

Delight and desire may seem friendly, but because they are not under your control, they can't be "good." Confusing them with genuine good only leads to suffering and anxiety. Anguish and fear seem unpleasant, but because they are not under your control, they cannot be "bad." Thinking of them as terrible leads to suffering and anxiety.

None of the four passions are good or bad in themselves. They only become good or bad because of the false beliefs that people have about them, leading people to invest all their hopes for happiness in aspects of life that they cannot control.

good feelings

The goal of stoic practice is apatheia, which means to be "pathos-free." Although this sounds like "apathy" and is the origin of the word, apatheia's original meaning is to be free of painful emotions, not all feelings. Instead of pathos, the stoic experiences "good feelings" or apatheia. A "good feeling" in the stoic sense is one that no one and nothing can take away from you because it is based on things that are under your control.

The Stoics recognized three apatheia: joy, caution, and desire. The three good feelings have something in common with the four types of pathos. However, unlike Delight, Desire, Distress, and fear's violent passions, the three good feelings are calm and relaxed. Joy is the quiet and serene enjoyment of something you prefer, without the irrational attachment of pathos. Caution is rational and dignified self-control, with which the stoic faces danger or makes decisions about his health, without the sadness of irrational fear. Desiring is the reasonable anticipation of future Joy, without the grasping quality of irrational desire.

PATHOS	**GOOD FEELING**
Delight	Joy

Fear	Caution
Wish	Wishing

As you can see, the good feelings of a stoic are very similar to those of an average person, with a big difference. The Stoic is calmly happy in all conditions, while the ordinary person constantly struggles with negative feelings. By focusing your happiness on your own decisions, you can experience the good feels of Stoicism while avoiding the emotional storms of pathos.

Chapter 5: General Misconceptions about Stoicism

To overturn your thinking system, which is critical if you want stoic logic to be effective in helping you achieve the goals you have set, it is essential to examine the most common preconceived notions that people have about stoic philosophy. I talked about some before, but here, let's be more specific. I will start with the most common ones and build from there.

a.   That Stoicism is too austere.
I think this opinion arose from the first years of Stoicism, a time when cynicism was in fashion. The cynical way of life was to renounce any worldly possession and live a godly life. Although the early Stoic teachers made a clear distinction in this regard, it has taken a while for their differentiation to be realized.
It's also quite possible that the absence of an extravagant lifestyle typical of most Stoics makes it seem like they are not having fun or enjoying life. The truth of this is simple: Stoic logic teaches you not to value wealth and material things. Therefore materialism does not quickly move you. Instead, he appreciates the contributions made in his life, but this does not control his actions.

a.   That Stoicism is a religious sect.
In the early years, Stoicism had a cult following, which probably instigated the idea that it was a religious sect. However, more than being a religion, it is a way of thinking and reasoning. Unlike religions, where you are required to adopt all facets, Stoicism allows you to take certain elements and apply them in a way that seems best to you.
In the application of stoic logic, a deity does not dictate your dealings in life. What you eat, how you dress, and what you do is dictated by your sense of right and wrong. However, your perspective is not the only factor in the decision-making process. You should also consider how your actions can affect your relationships with others.

a.   That Stoicism means withdrawing from the world.
To practice Stoicism, you don't have to give up your daily job, sell your house, and settle in a hidden monastery. You don't need to contemplate the mysteries of the universe from the silence of a cave, and you certainly don't need to make a vow of silence just to be able to activate the voice of emotional reasoning.

There are many people, both past and present, who actively participated in their communities and maintained a vibrant social life. However, they were staunch Stoics or, at the very least, practiced Stoic principles. If you need to take time off from the pressures of life, do it by all means. This is a primary human need. But don't ignore the other fundamental human need to connect, either. The key is balance.

a.   Stoics have no emotions.

This may fall within the scope of the first misconception on the list, but I had to separate this from austerity because of its importance to our daily lives. The average human experiences a variety of emotions. Some of these emotions are very uplifting, while others crush the soul. In the broader scheme of things, some of these emotions are the biological defense of our body against threats to our person.

Choosing to live without these emotional experiences is the exact opposite of what Stoicism teaches. Pain helps you cope with loss, fear keeps you alert to danger, and even anger serves to strengthen you to protect you. Stoic logic allows you to experience these emotions but trains you to avoid letting your actions dictate, even when you are in your most hectic state, your efforts will be guided by rational thinking.

Sure, the average stoic isn't going to have a tantrum when the waiter mixes his order. That doesn't mean he wasn't mad about it. You simply choose to react in a way that is most productive for the situation. So if by chance you signed up for this because you hoped to become a stubborn human, you may need to rethink your options.

a.   Stoicism is difficult

I think this is more an old thing. We're so used to life at the push of a button that is going through items that require a process that can seem tedious. You want to enter your meditation corner, connect your thumb to your finger, take a deep breath, and exhale all your troubles.

Stoicism does not work that way. This is a lifelong process. Every day is lived with a conscientious effort to take into account everything we do. If you hope to correct certain behaviors, develop your confidence, and live a good life, you will have to get used to applying stoic logic every day.

a.   The practice of Stoicism eliminates your free will.

Stoic logic encompasses the role that destiny plays in our lives. This essentially means that you have to accept your place and station in life. Most people have interpreted this to say that we are expected to turn around and play dead under the circumstances only; This could not be more wrong.

Stoic logic advocates that people analyze their situation objectively. In explaining what is happening, they can truly understand what is under their control and what is not. This type of thinking puts them in harmony with the situation because they have acquired an idea of the true nature of what they are facing. And it is with this knowledge that they can take steps that will bring the most desirable results.

Chapter 6: Stoicism in everyday life

Practicing Stoicism in modern times is not that different from being a Christian, a Buddhist, or practicing the customs and beliefs that prevail in your community. It is not a religion. However, it is a way of life. Practitioners simply reflect on the teachings and then try as much as possible to engage their minds with themes and thoughts that offer better options. Stoics are more proactive about their daily lives: They don't lie down, wake up, and wait for life to happen to them while doing their daytime activities. Instead, they do their best to anticipate the challenges of the day and plan actions for those challenges.

They meditate on the four cardinal virtues of strength, justice, temperance, and prudence, and try to imagine how they will have to use them that day. This does not mean that they can predict the events of the day. However, they can be programmed to handle better the surprises that life will bring. The "programming" of the stoic mind is done by participating in different stoic exercises, which may include imagining the worst-case scenario for the day. Here, the Stoics think about the worst event that could happen that day, then develop their mentality to be indifferent to this tragedy. This exercise is called Hierocles' circle.

This does not necessarily mean that the Stoics want this tragedy to occur. We prefer those good things to happen to us. But this type of training puts your mind in a state where you can remove your sense of worth and self-esteem from the event. If you are like most people, your greatest fear would be the loss of your livelihood. With the standard mindset, a loss like that could trigger depression, panic, and other negative emotions that can trigger adverse reactions. This exercise helps you eliminate that fear. So even if it happens, you can live above this crisis.

For some people, this type of thinking may seem morbid, especially if their worst fear is death. Often these fears prevent us from living our daily lives. I know of a woman who barely escaped her marriage through the skin of her teeth due to her abusive husband. With the help of friends and family, she was able to bring him to justice and send him to prison. It was a temporary victory for her because her sentence became a countdown clock that caused her to experience anxiety and panic attacks.

She would jump from her dream in a state of fright, thinking that that day would be the day that her husband would walk free. She couldn't accept jobs, she was afraid to buy a house, and she couldn't even enjoy a dull moment with the family because, at any moment, her ex-husband could walk through the door. She practiced the Hierocles circular exercise. In those moments of meditation, he unearthed every horrible version of his nightmare. Where she was dragged by her hair on the streets, where he murdered her in her sleep, it was bloody, and, in the initial stages, it was baffling.

But she went on with it. In his own words, the visions became less terrifying over time until he found himself trying to invent more terrifying scenarios to increase fear. However, the truth was that she had lived through her worst fears, and this opened a new door for her. She enrolled in self-defense classes, not because she wanted to fight but because it helped her feel more secure. He approached his family and became more open to his friends. The paralysis imposed by fear ceased the moment she overcame her fears. This is just one example of how Stoicism can be applied in your life.

Another significant benefit of practicing Stoicism is its ability to help you focus on the present. There are many things around us in life: so many passions, so many dreams, so many opportunities, and, along the same lines, so many fears. Tomorrow's uncertainty is what drives many of us to a fundamental level. The ability to pay those substantial, recurring bills has us sitting at our desks day after day, working at jobs that don't interest us. We settle for relationships that cause us more harm than good because we are afraid of being alone.

In situations where we must defend our rights, we allow our fears to silence us, but more than anything, we spend our days worrying. We are concerned with what could have been, what should have been, and what would have been. Some of us care more about the past. Mistakes and actions are taken previously, haunt us, and prevent us from enjoying what is happening now. So you have people who are precisely the opposite: they live in the moment, but for the wrong reasons.

These are the people who live only by their desires and passions. They should buy that new fall coat. They must have the latest phone. If everyone is doing it, it should be okay if they do it too. It is like throwing beads along a rope that has no end. They just keep choosing one account after another. Never experience happiness, never genuinely enjoy the moment. All they do is want more. This is the ruin of living in these modern times. The practice of Stoicism can keep you in the present. Seneca put it this way:

"The greatest blessings of humanity are within us and within our reach. A wise man is a content with his lot, whatever it may be, without desiring what he does not have.

It is not necessary to embrace Stoicism in its entirety. You can do stoic exercises that you think will bring you closer to your goals. In the rest of the chapters, I will share some of these exercises and offer guides to help you integrate them into your daily routine.

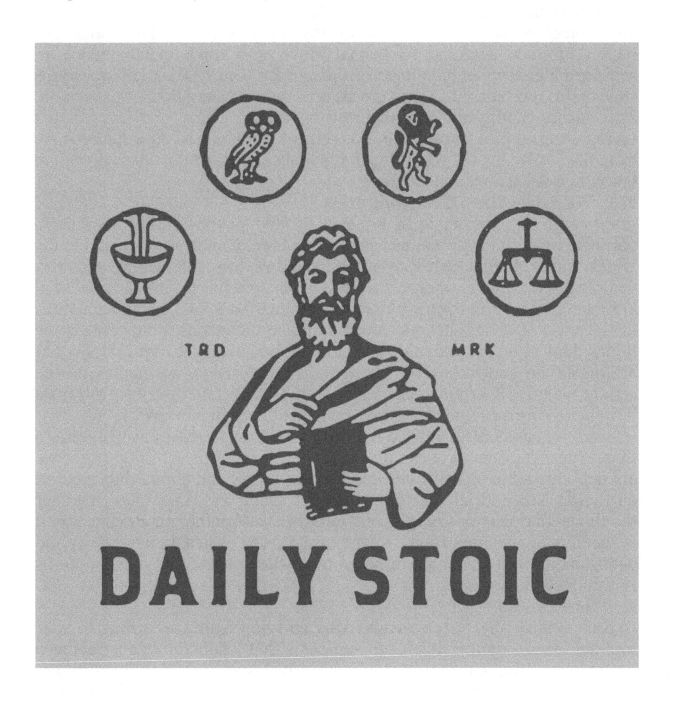

Chapter 7: APPLICATION TO STOISM WITH DAILY LIFE

Stoicism has many vital principles that, when combined, makeup what Stoicism is all about.

For Stoics, the most crucial goal of any life was to be eudemonia. Put merely, Stoics believes that the primary purpose of any human being was to achieve a high level of happiness or satisfaction. One of the main questions stoic philosophy sought to answer was how to live a good life.

a.   Living in unity and accordance with nature

Living according to nature was the central principle of Stoic philosophy from the beginning. He advocates that people behave rationally, rather than trying to rebel against the universe.

a.   Focus on what you can control

Another primary principle of Stoicism is that people must differentiate between what they can control and what they cannot, and focus on the issues under their control. Without making this distinction, we risk worrying about things where our concern has no impact. This is considered a waste of effort and contrary to stoic practice. To quote Epictetus, "Make the best use of what is in your power and take the rest as it happens. Some things depend on us, and others do not." In our lives, the main things that are under our control are our thoughts. , the decisions we make and the actions we take. Everything else in existence is not under our control. Even if we try to control some of these external problems in our favor,

Instead, we can control our thoughts, decisions, and actions in response to these external events. We can decide if we are satisfied with them or if we are not. This act of focusing on what we can control and ignore that is out of our hands is beneficial because it helps us spend less time agonizing over the things that may be going wrong in our lives. Another significant way it is useful is to give importance to our reactions to external phenomena and determine how to feel about these events, which means that our happiness is ultimately in our hands.

a.   Live by virtue

In Stoic philosophy, virtue means living and flourishing according to your rational human nature. What this means is that when you live a balanced life, you are living a pleasant experience. The Stoics classified the different types of virtue into four: wisdom, justice, courage, and self-discipline. When you act by these virtues, you gradually move towards eudemony, which is considered the ultimate goal of life. For someone to count as virtuous in Stoic philosophy, you have to practice all the virtues consistently. If one of these virtues is left unfulfilled, the person does not count as a virtuous person. In Stoic philosophy, being virtuous was considered, in itself, the reward for acts of virtue.

4. Distinguish between good, bad, and indifferent things.

For Stoics, the good things are the four cardinal virtues: justice, wisdom, self-discipline, and courage. The bad things are the opposites of the virtues, namely: injustice, foolishness, indulgence, and cowardice. The final set is indifferent things like pleasure and pain, life and death, etc. In Stoic philosophy, indifferent things are those that do not directly harm or help our attempts to be virtuous people. For example, a sick person may be moral, while a healthy person may also lack virtue. Indifferent things are those that have no direct relationship with the type of person we are. As such, Stoic philosophy advocates that people should be indifferent to these things. However,

a. Take action

For Stoics, most of the things that happen in life are out of their control and are still no excuse for them to sit down and do nothing. It is not an excuse for them to be indifferent to how they live their lives. Instead, Stoics believe that the event's results in their lives still depend heavily on their actions. While you are not in control of external affairs, you can control your efforts to achieve the desired result. Stoics believe that events are not prewritten to go a certain way, regardless of what you do. Instead, they are required to follow the actions you take. As such, the results of the events happening around you still depend significantly on the steps you have taken towards that event.

You may not control the outcome, but you control your actions, so if your plan is just to give up and leave everything to "fate," you will find yourself unable to achieve the good life you want with force, and you will not be able the objective. The good life means that you will not be the right person. Although the Stoics consider that the things that happen outside them are indifferent, they still do not take it as an excuse for not acting in a calculated way towards achieving the goals they want.

a. Love everything that happens

This part of Stoic doctrine advocates that people love whatever happens to them, regardless of whether they like it. Often people spend a lot of time bogged down by the events in their lives and begin to feel negative about it. Usually, these are things that happened in the past, but still always upset people for their experiences. The stoic way to overcome this is to love every event that happens in your life. Change your mind about the things that happen in your life, regardless of whether they happened in your favor or not, like when they came. These events cannot be changed, so there is no point in looking at them. Instead, turn your opinion about them.

To some extent, you may even decide to enjoy the things that happen to you because you have come to accept them as part of your life and journey. While it may be an exaggeration to expect us to be grateful for the things in our life that we never wanted, you should consider that they are part of a "bigger plan" that is forming in your life. That way, when something happens in your life that you don't immediately approve of, you can reconsider it and begin to see it as just another part of your journey to happiness.

a.   Understand that plans change

As Stoics, the belief is that your actions, thoughts, and feelings are the only things under your control. You are always supposed to do the right thing and do everything possible to achieve this goal. However, the Stoic doctrine teaches that you must be willing to change paths if your preferred outcome does not happen. We must do everything possible to do good and succeed, but we must not forget that some things can happen that prevent our plans or the desired results from happening.

The Stoics believed that the wise are always prepared for anything that happens. Quoting Seneca, "nothing happens to the wise against his expectations." A wise man would have prepared himself for any possible outcome, so if things go for or against him, it is already expected, and the wise man already has a plan to follow. Whenever you plan to do something, always keep things that may prevent you from achieving the goals you have in mind.

Always do your best, considering that the result is not under your control. When you finally get the result, accept it as it is, regardless of whether it is what you wanted. From there, as before, continue to seek to do good and achieve virtue. As soon as you see the result, start adjusting to the effect, to make the most of your new circumstances and act with decency in the future.

This is called having a reservation clause because you try to achieve something while understanding that problems can arise that prevent you from doing what you planned. Having this clause helps you spend less time overthinking what you should have done differently. You already understand that achieving your plans depended on things going precisely according to your project.

8. Consider your obstacles to be opportunities.

In everything you do, always take the obstacles you face and consider them opportunities. A useful tool for this is your perception of the events in your life. Your knowledge of events dramatically affects how you view the world around you. The way you see things around you has a significant impact on how you live your life. Stoics have learned to display events that occur outside them as good or bad, but as indifferent. This means that these events are mostly unimportant, but the important part is how we view these events. Stoics believe that what matters is not the external events occurring, but how we think or perceive them. So, you have no control over these external events,

To help them do this, Stoics tries to assess the situation as objectively as possible and then decide to see and make the best of the current situation. This is how you can turn what is initially presented as an obstacle on your way into a barrier that you can use to your advantage, making it an opportunity. The key to identifying these obstacles that can become opportunities lies a lot in your perception. The sooner your understanding of events in your life changes, the faster you can begin to turn those obstacles into opportunities. In this way, you can make the most of every situation you are in.

a.   Be aware

At the heart of Stoic doctrine is the need to be vigilant at all times. In everything you do, you must remain conscious and aware of your actions. If you are going to live according to virtue as in Stoic doctrine, you must continue mindful of everything you do. Staying aware of yourself and the things around you helps you stay in reality, allowing you to make rational decisions. You must continually control your thoughts, feelings, and emotions to avoid acting irrationally. When monitoring your beliefs, you can stay on track and make thoughtful practical decisions.

You cannot practice Stoicism if you cannot stay vigilant. In turn, the more you practice patience, the better you will be aware. Being aware also helps you measure your reaction to the events around you and make the best decisions, rather than instinctively reacting to external events and stimuli. Mindfulness not only allows you to understand your actions but also helps you understand the emotion that drives that action. If you don't recognize this, it may be difficult for you to evolve. Your feelings, emotions, thoughts, and activities are the only things you can control, so you should keep them in mind. Mindfulness does not only include being present in your life and considering events as they occur so that you can develop a reaction. It also involves reflecting on past events and your response to them, so that you can determine the things you did well and the mistakes you made that do not reveal your chosen Stoic lifestyle. This helps you to be a better stoic in the future. You could also write your thoughts about the day, in the same way, that Marco Aurelio did in his Meditations.

a.   Practice misfortune

A common practice among Stoics is to practice misfortune to prepare for anything that could go wrong. It was one of the primary motivations for the creation of the Stoic movement. It was a way for people to learn to remain calm despite things in the present, not to go their way. Visualizing the possible misfortune that could happen was a way of preparing coping strategies in advance, just in case they did not get the results they wanted. Also known as negative visualization. Because the Stoics considered these things to be indifferent, practicing misfortune helped them prepare their coping strategies before the likelihood that the accident they had envisioned would occur.

Eventually, the goal was to build a level of disregard for these possible misfortunes that would allow people to face these misfortunes, if they occurred, most rationally and naturally possible, rather than freaking out or being disappointed when they happened. Stoicism teaches people to be ready for a different outcome than they would like or prefer to see happen. It shows always to be prepared to change plans and avoid stopping in misfortune if they become real.

Chapter 8: Living according to nature

Every stoic thinker believes in the motto: "live according to nature." In his meditations, Marco Aurelio, the Stoic Emperor, explained this belief saying that "philosophy will only require what its nature already demands." Zeno, the founder of Stoicism in the other nature defined as "the way things work" and therefore requires only wisdom to act by natural laws. Seneca, another stoic, explains that "as humans, we must follow the path that nature has laid out for us. If humans follow nature, everything will be smooth, and without obstacles. However, if we fight nature, then there is no difference between us and those who row against the current. " In other words, all these thoughts from Emperor Marcus Aurelius,

Well, to any reader who grasps Stoicism, I know this sounds strange. However, the stoic prescription believes that human nature is impulsive and selfish. Therefore, what the Stoics had in mind was generally above the natural base impulses seen in healthy humans. The greatest gift that nature gave humans was the power to reason, and this is what separated humans from thoughtless animals. Here are the stoic rules that will help and guide you to live according to nature.

Focus on what's at your fingertips
It is only by first accepting our natural limitations (both inherent and circumstantial limitations) that we can live according to nature. The laws that govern life and nature, whether good or bad, cannot be changed by humans. In any case that we want to live undisturbed, we must quickly accept this fact. Freedom can only come once we understand the limits of our power as humans and the natural boundaries that divine dispositions have established. The moment we accept the restrictions and inevitability in our lives; We learn to work with these limits and inevitability instead of fighting against it. By doing so, we become free.

Therefore, evaluate your thoughts and feelings to understand your natural talents and affinities better. Build on who you are, and be sure to make the most of it. Never push yourself for things that are entirely beyond your current capabilities because this will end up frustrating you. When a man is in harmony with himself, man pursues limited natural desires. The desire for more (greed) that the Stoic describes as unnatural cannot be satisfied. This means that if you are a person looking for things beyond your control, for example, something like wealth, physical pleasure, or reputation, you will end up being a very frustrated person. Seneca speaks of this by pointing out that poverty and wealth are relative concepts. When a man chooses to restrain himself within limits set by nature, such a man will not notice poverty. However, when a man exceeds the limits set by nature, he will be haunted by poverty, regardless of how rich he may be.

Philosophy is a way of life.
The philosopher Epictetus urges us always to have the courage to approach our daily activities with the same degree of seriousness and discipline that soldiers or singers show during their training. Regardless of whether a matter is small and domestic or large and public, always behave according to the laws of nature. Your best treatment should always ensure that you harmonize your will with nature. Practice this ideal in your own daily life and your tasks and duties. Aristotle believes that his virtue is defined by his habit and not by an isolated act. The best way to absorb Stoic principles can only be through ethical practices. Both desire and aversion can be considered powerful habits. However, we can train ourselves to develop and have better habits.

Avoid habits that make you want to chase things that are not under your control. We should also focus on combating things that are not good for us and within our power. Each individual has their weaknesses and inclinations. The most effective way we can counter characters' flaws is by opposing those characters with contrary habits. In the same way, the way we engage in fear of pain or extreme physical pleasure, we must also train at opposite ends of what we love.

Demonstrate absolute commitment to truth
When you choose to live according to nature's requirements, prepare to be committed to the truth. There is nothing good that can come from superstitious beliefs, fear, illusions, or greed. The worst thing of all you can do is to lie to yourself. Lying to yourself will separate you from your instincts. This is what results in a feeling of disconnection. The Stoic teaches that we must develop in ourselves an attitude of complete honesty, especially towards oneself. Absolute commitment to truth means that in every thought, every word/expression, and in every moment of life.

Open your eyes and learn to see things as they are, as this will save you the pain caused by avoidable devastation and malicious attachments. Regardless of how we perceive people and things or how they seem to us, the fact is that they will continue to be what they are. Therefore, instead of turning our eyes away from the painful events in our lives, we should look at them properly and think about them frequently. When we face real events caused by disappointment, death, or illness, we are freed from illusions and false hopes. In this way, we avoid being miserable or envious thoughts.

See adversity as a challenge and an opportunity.
Adversity tests the honesty we have with ourselves. We have to face trouble because it is part of nature. You will be considered ignorant of half of the view if you claim to be always lucky that you have never gone through life with never known pain. Through adversity, we discover our mettle. We must accept the challenges of misfortune. When we face difficulties in life, we are presented with the opportunity to draw on our inner being and invoke the internal resources immersed in us. We can only know our strengths from the tests we endure.

Chapter 9: The Science of Letting Go of the Past and Living in the Present

Leave the past behind by cutting off any attachments you have, especially with painful memories. Memories may be dragging you without your knowledge. Forget about your past pain, and start accepting what the future holds for you. You must fight against the past and stop getting discouraged or disappointed. Get on with life and make things go as they should. Release the thoughts that accumulate in you, the habits, the fears, and the worries. Stay away from past emotions that make you resentful so you can face the future as an active person. If you do not abandon the past, you will suffer bad relationships, jealousy, and envy. Letting go requires you to have a determination and work daily in your life.

There are things you can involve in your daily practice so that you can leave that past behind and have a good future. They include and are not limited to;

Making peace with the past

It is time for you to accept that what happened at that moment belongs to the past and not to the future. Don't let that depress or bind you to the point where you can't live a healthy future. Thinking about the bad things that have happened will not help you in any way. That will do you more harm than good. Although your mind will continue to bring back painful memories, you must replace them with positive ones with immediate effect. Be smart and creative in countering any negative thoughts that may want to remind you of what you did in the past. Teach your mind to think of a positive tomorrow when the past tries to haunt you. That will quickly become a habit, and you will eventually find yourself letting go of the range you have. You can practice mindfulness as a technique to replace negative thoughts. When you bring your focus to the present, The past will have a minor impact on its future. Practice living in the present, and you'll hurt yourself less and be in a position to control it. You are free to choose the things you want in life, and you have to make a wise decision to live the life of your expectations.

Face your fears

Fear may be what keeps you from letting go of your past. To continue a healthy life, you must face your worries and disappointments. Cut your connection to fear, and you will succeed in life. You have to keep trying, and eventually, you will. People will often be afraid of grief, sadness, anger, and disappointment. Don't dismiss such feelings; instead, give them a chance to get out of you. When you decide to fight them, you will be trapped, and it will be difficult for you to move on. Don't avoid negative emotions from the past, as that will make you dwell in the past. Naturally, a person will find a way to counter any pain that comes their way. Spending most of your time trying to distract your feelings will not initiate a disconnect. Finding something you like to do so you don't think about the past won't pay off. You should know that the more you do it, the more you will hurt yourself. Focusing on such things will only drain your energy. When you feel like you can't do it alone, find someone you think will help you get through the past.

Practice being gentle with yourself
Show yourself compassion and kindness so that the past stops tormenting you. Don't criticize yourself when you find yourself in a painful situation. Treat yourself the same way you would treat the person you love. If you don't love yourself, you will have a hard time dealing with the past, which means your future will be full of bruises. Although pain is not inevitable in any way, treat yourself with love and kindness if it does come. Practice self-care once you are hurt, and that will be one way to set clear boundaries. Say no to things that bother you and do things that bring you joy and comfort that don't forget to manage your needs first. When you learn to implement self-care daily, you will empower yourself, and there will be an overwhelming feeling. Focus on yourself and address the accumulated resentment in you. Try to bring yourself to the present whenever you feel your thoughts drift into the past. Pay attention to the things you are grateful for and not what hurts you.

Don't expect an apology.
You know you are firm when you accept an apology from someone who has hurt you and does not apologize. Waiting for someone to apologize is the worst mistake you'll ever make. That will slow you down by letting go of the past, and in most cases, that person doesn't care what happens to their future. Don't wait for them to take care of your healing - instead, you need to take care of their healing process. The pain and the pain accumulated in you do not affect the person who hurt you but transforms you. Don't wait for the person to apologize. Don't expect them to. When you do that, you will speed up your healing, and faster, you can release it. Work on your forgiveness as waiting for them to apologize will stop the whole process.
Be free to talk about it.

Going through tough times, you need to find someone you can talk to about it. When you speak it, it will be a way to help you heal, and you will let it go. When you don't talk about it, you will never get better, and living in the past will delay your life. Don't feel embarrassed or as if it's embarrassing to talk about it with the people around you. Find someone patient enough with you and willing to offer you the help you can get so you can leave the past behind. You can also seek professional advice once you feel like you don't have anyone you can trust. When you talk to a therapist, the struggle to quit will lessen, and eventually, you will. When you meet a professional with experience in such matters, they will guide you on implementing the process.

Practice mindfulness
Practicing mindfulness is a way to train the brain to live in the present and focus its awareness on the senses and not on the thoughts. Focus your attention on the things that are happening right now. Leave what happened some time ago alone and let it remain as history. Aim to notice every activity that is and let the mind float without any attachment. Make it a practice, and it will be easy for you to refocus your thoughts on what is happening in the present. Find a starting point and start so you can leave the past behind. It can be challenging to do, but once you can practice that, you will find that ideas are flowing in the right direction.

Create a distance
It will be helpful if you create a gap between the person or the situation, which continually reminds you of the past. Whatever you are doing, your discomfort should not be near you. It is not wrong to put a physical distance from the person who is making you live in your past. Also, create a psychological range from any circumstance that takes you back to the past. You should avoid anyone who advises you that fighting the past will not help you in any way. No one should discourage you from processing the past, as it will be an excellent way to heal.

Be creative
Creativity, when it comes to real life, is a way of leaving your past behind. When you engage your mind in creating new beginnings and things, you will have less time to dwell on the past. Open your thoughts to new opportunities and do the things that will make you happy. Seek to meet new

people when those with you discourage you from moving in that direction. You must accept the change every time it is presented to you. Take a different course and orientation when things seem to change. It will work for you since change is as good as rest. Yearn to discover more, and that will help you release the anger you feel in you because of your past mistakes.

Work with a positive attitude.
You need to create affirmative phrases that you need to remember once the painful past tries to find away. How you speak to yourself will determine whether you will move forward or continue moving backward. The more you talk positively with yourself, the more you can leave the past behind. You can often rephrase your mind when you practice a mantra that you will say to yourself when you are in a painful and emotional moment. Train your mind to think about the possible and not the impossible. That way, you will move forward more efficiently and forget how the future treated you. Bring people together who see what's right in you. You should also focus on your strengths rather than your weaknesses.

You should know that both positive and negative experiences in your life will help shape the future. You will meet people, situations, and events that will determine who you will be in the coming days. Note that you will not focus on the negatives and those that will hurt you. That will help you get through any experiences that are similar to those of the past. And you will not be partial. You will be hit by mental blindness when you decide to focus only on the negative side. Spending all your time fighting against impossibility will link your spiritual resources and keep you away from a good life. You will make a difference in how you will deal with the painful past. Keep in mind that emotional pain will keep you away from healing.

You need to simplify your life so that the unforeseen consequences do not affect you. Living in the past will only steal your current joy. Choose to live in the future, and you will find it exciting and have a healthy and meaningful life. Live in the present moment, and the future will have a smooth flow.
When you learn to leave the past behind, seek to know how you need to live. Concentrate on living in the present. Leaving the past behind is not only an important thing, but living resentment is a wise decision. Crying over the past will make you worry about both the present and the future. It will always make you anticipate problems, and you will have a hard time coping with life. Aim for the best, and you'll find it enjoyable living in the present

moment. Make a conscious decision and control every situation by celebrating every little achievement you make.

Chapter 10: stoicism and psychology

All have not welcomed the renewed popularity of Stoicism. Stoicism is sometimes criticized as an outdated philosophy, a relic of ancient thought with no place in the modern world. Some people say that it is not realistic that we cannot control our emotions by merely changing our belief system. Other people say that we shouldn't even try and that Stoicism would prevent us from experiencing love or joy. Does Stoicism increase good feelings as its practitioners claim, or does the rejection of passions lead to a gray life without emotional depth?

Like Epictetus, the great Stoics taught us that our thoughts are the primary source of our happiness and unhappiness in life. So how well does stoicism match what we know about the brain? If stoic ideas have any validity, they should be confirmed by modern psychology and cognitive science.

There are many different therapies in psychology, ranging from traditional Freudian psychotherapy to acceptance and commitment therapy. One of the most effective and widely used treatments is known as cognitive-behavioral therapy or CBT.

CBT is used to treat anxiety, mood disorders, eating disorders, depression, addiction to gambling, substance abuse, and many other common problems. Studies have shown that it is one of the most effective and practical types of therapy, and is considered the preferred treatment for a wide range of cognitive and behavioral problems. Studies have shown that it is as effective as medication in some cases, making it the ideal choice for people who want to address their issues without medicines.

Although CBT is a treatment method rather than a philosophy, the central ideas of this therapy are based on ancient Stoicism. Practicing Stoicism is not the same as receiving cognitive behavioral therapy treatment from a qualified professional, and receiving CBT treatment will not make you a philosopher. The two are different. However, the tools that CBT therapists use are based on the ideas of Epictetus, Seneca, and Marco Aurelio, a compelling argument for the validity of the Stoic worldview.

Cognitive-behavioral therapy is a broad term, encompassing several different methods. Emotional, cognitive behavioral therapy, structured cognitive-behavioral training, moral reconciliation therapy, stress inoculation training, unified protocol, mindfulness-based cognitive behavioral hypnotherapy, and brief cognitive behavioral therapy are all types of CBT.

All of these therapies have slightly different theories and techniques, and some incorporate other influences along with Stoicism. For example, mindfulness-based cognitive behavioral hypnotherapy includes some ideas from Buddhism. However, the basic concepts and assumptions of CBT are shared by all variations, and they all share the same roots in ancient Stoicism.

TCC development
CBT dates back to an earlier method called Cognitive Therapy, which is now considered one of the CBT subtypes. Cognitive therapy was developed in the 1960s by a psychoanalyst named Aaron Beck, who felt that traditional psychotherapy was too focused on the unconscious to be practical for most patients.

Beck's reading of the Stoics had convinced him that psychological problems are often influenced by how people think and what they believe about the world. This coincides with several passages in the Meditations of Marco Aurelio, where the emperor reminds himself that our beliefs and opinions are the leading cause of all our actions.

According to Beck, negative feelings and behaviors are often the direct consequence of negative beliefs and thoughts. I wanted to help patients recognize distorted thinking patterns so that they could transform them over time into more positive and functional thinking patterns. Beck believed that this would naturally lead to a decrease in dysfunctional behaviors, making cognitive therapy an effective treatment for substance abuse and other behavioral problems.

Cognitive therapy is based on Beck's cognitive model, which divides human thinking into three categories: automatic thoughts, shared beliefs, and central beliefs. Automatic thoughts are involuntary adverse reactions based on the patient's underlying assumptions about himself, other people, or the future.

For example, a person with an eating disorder may feel revulsion and self-hatred when looking in a mirror, imagining that he is much more substantial than he is. Automatic thoughts derive from common beliefs in an "if-then" pattern, for example, "if I lose enough weight, I will finally be popular." Shared beliefs are derived from core beliefs, such as "nobody likes me." By tracing automatic thinking to the core of the view that ultimately inspired it, it becomes clear that this patient's eating disorder is based on a deep conviction that it is unpleasant and that treating this belief is key to treating behavior.

In cognitive therapy, the therapist helps the patient learn to recognize automatic thoughts, then identifies the common and central beliefs that drive automatic thoughts. By asking a series of questions (a method borrowed from Socrates), the therapist demonstrates these beliefs' irrational nature.
Finally, the therapist helps the patient understand that these automatic beliefs and thoughts are distorted and inaccurate.

This process reflects the stoic approach to cognition, in which automatic reactions or "impressions" are questioned and only "nod" if they appear rational by Stoic standards. Primarily, the cognitive therapist teaches the patient to ask their impressions and to consent only to those who turn out to be sensible after close examination. Epictetus would undoubtedly approve.

Cognitive-behavioral therapy takes the basic idea of cognitive therapy. It adds behavioral techniques, especially the use of desensitization and conditioning techniques to help patients overcome neuroses such as phobias. The cognitive aspect of CBT is the aspect most influenced by Stoic philosophy. Still, the behavioral element has proven to be very useful for patients suffering from deep underlying fears and compulsions.
Thoughts, emotions, and actions.
In the CBT model of how the mind works, thoughts influence emotions, and emotions influence actions or behaviors. Our efforts confirm our beliefs about the world, and the cycle repeats itself.
For example, you might think that you cannot relax and relax without a little wine. This thought makes you feel stressed and tense until you drink some wine, at which point you feel a little more relaxed. The next time you have the same thought, you are more likely to act accordingly because of

your experience of drinking the wine confirmed the validity of the idea. Of course, drinking too much wine causes other problems over time, but it's hard to get out of the circle because the connection between theory, feeling, and action seems compelling. Even if you suspect that drinking too much is causing you a lot more stress, it's hard for you to accept that it won't help you.

On a deeper level, CBT holds that our core beliefs drive our thoughts. Like cognitive therapy, core beliefs fall into three categories: beliefs about self, opinions about other people, and feelings about the world. For example, the idea that it is not possible to relax without wine may be driven by fundamental assumptions that the world is a dangerous and stressful place, that other people cannot or will not offer emotional support, and that no one can be trusted except yourself when you feel overwhelmed. Not knowing different ways to relax effectively, he convinces himself that drinking wine is the only realistic option.

This is just a simplified version of how CBT works, but Stoicism's connection is easy to see. Epictetus would undoubtedly agree that our core beliefs about the world inform our opinions about specific situations, generate negative emotions or paths, such as fear, and ultimately lead us to make unhealthy decisions. Stoicism and cognitive behavioral therapy share the same underlying and practical assumption that our actions are based primarily on what we believe about the world. The most effective way to make positive changes in our lives is to change what we think. However, CBT does not focus on the central doctrine of Stoicism that all cognitive distortions ultimately come from the same source.

Cognitive distortions
The main difference between the stoic approach and the CBT approach is in defining what makes a thought "distorted" or useless. In classical Stoicism, setting something outside your control as "good" or "bad" is a cognitive distortion. This is the fundamental mistake that the Stoic wants to avoid. In CBT, there are four types of cognitive distortion: catastrophize, overgeneralize, minimize positives, and maximize negatives.

Catastrophization is a type of if-then thinking in which the worst-case scenario is supposed to be true. For example, "If I don't keep my house spotlessly clean, I will get sick and die" or "If I don't get this complete report, I will be fired, and my career will be ruined. "

Excessive generalization is coming to a radical conclusion without enough evidence to support the end. For example, if you go to a party and no one talks to you, it would be an excessive generalization to assume that no one likes you or wants to talk to you. His experience at a single party is not enough evidence for generalization.

Minimizing the positives is the habit of ignoring any evidence that things are going well for you. For example, it may be said that your new promotion doesn't matter because you will simply feel overwhelmed by stress and ruin things.

Maximizing the negative is the habit of focusing too much on what's difficult or challenging. For example, it can be said that he is alone because he has no girlfriend, ignoring the fact that he has several close friends.

The four cognitive distortions of CBT show some influence of Stoicism. Marco Aurelio and Epictetus warn us that we should not allow ourselves to think "what would happen if," but that we stick to the basic facts about the situation. It is not harmful to say, "my mother is sick," but it is detrimental to say, "my mother is sick; what if she dies? Avoid thinking," what would happen if "you avoid catastrophe.

Sticking to the facts is also a good defense against excessive generalization. "I went to the party, and nobody spoke to me" is just a fact, without any value judgment. "I went to the party, and nobody spoke to me because nobody wants to speak to me," is an excessive generalization. By merely adding nothing to the objective account, you can avoid this type of cognitive distortion.

The other two types of cognitive distortion are a little further from stoic thought because a stoic would never admit that any external event could be positive or negative in the first place. Minimizing positives would simply be "minimizing indifferent favorites," and maximizing negatives would simply be "maximizing indifferent favorites." The stoic way of thinking about life gives no real importance to either of them.

That is the difference between Stoicism as philosophy and CBT as therapy. To practice patience, you must accept Stoic teachings about what matters and what doesn't. Without taking that virtue is the only good, it would be challenging to practice Stoicism. To benefit from CBT, you do not have to accept any particular belief. You just have to be willing to question your existing ideas with the therapist's help and guidance.

Cognitive-behavioral therapy is a practical application of stoic ideas for people who don't necessarily know anything about Stoicism.

Stages of cognitive-behavioral therapy
Cognitive-behavioral therapy begins with an evaluation, in which the therapist attempts to determine what critical behaviors are affecting the client's life. Then the therapist decides whether these behaviors are excessive or deficient, too much, or too little for the actual situation. The therapist discovers how often the reaction occurs, how long it generally lasts, and how intense it is. This becomes the baseline, and the goal of therapy is to increase or decrease the frequency of behavior depending on the circumstances.

For example, the behavior could be excessive hand washing, a typical compulsive symptom. The therapist would discover how often the client washes their hands and how much time is spent doing it. The goal of therapy would be to reduce the frequency and duration of the behavior, so it stops causing problems in the client's life.

The next phase in CBT is reconceptualization, where the client is encouraged to think about their problem differently. This phase is similar to the Stoic approach in that it is based on changing the client's beliefs about the world.

This phase is followed by the acquisition of skills, where the patient practices specific exercises to help him modify the behavior. Once these skills are consolidated, the therapist helps the patient generalize what they have learned in therapy. By learning to detect the four fundamental cognitive distortions, the patient receives the tools to become his therapist in the future.

That does not mean that everything is going well from this point onwards. Patients generally need a few follow-up sessions to ensure they haven't fallen back into the old ways of thinking.

Stoicism in positive psychology

Of course, cognitive behavioral therapy only supports Stoicism in a limited way. The creators of CBT did not incorporate all aspects of patience into the effective treatments they were designing. CBT's success suggests that Stoicism is right on some key points, mainly that our beliefs primarily determine our happiness or unhappiness.

However, the effectiveness of CBT cannot be interpreted as evidence of Stoicism's most important claims. For that, psychologists would have to test endurance itself, not a therapy derived from tolerance. The purpose of treatment is to correct a disorder, but the goal of philosophy like Stoicism is to achieve well-being and happiness. This is the domain of positive psychology, a movement to redirect psychology from the exclusive study of psychological disorders and towards the education of human well-being. Some researchers in this field have decided to test whether Stoicism can fulfill their claims and improve people's lives.

In 2013 Professor Christopher Gill of the University of Exeter conducted a research study on Stoicism's benefits with Tim LeBon of the Modern Stoicism website. The study aimed to determine if stoic training would help participants experience more life satisfaction and more positive emotions.

Participants in the study were taught the basics of stoic practice and assigned a set of daily exercises. The exercises included a morning meditation on Stoic principles, a regular survey of the stoic tenets and techniques, a Stoic worksheet, and evening meditation on things that were done well and poorly during the day. All of these exercises were based on specific passages from the Stoic classics.

Some of the participants were recruited from existing stoic discussion groups, and others were recruited from the general public. The study lasted a single week, after which participants were asked a series of questions to determine what effect a one-week training course in Stoicism had on their daily lives.

By the end of the week, the number of life satisfaction reported by the participants increased by 14%. The frequency/intensity of negative emotion decreased by 11%, and the frequency/intensity of positive emotion increased by 9%. Feelings of optimism increased by 18%, and 56% of participants described themselves as behaving more ethically than usual. These are significant improvements for a study that lasted just a week, providing strong scientific support for Stoicism as a pathway to greater well-being, happiness, and virtue.

The Stoic Attitudes and Behavior Self-Assessment Scale

In an attempt to further study the relationship between Stoicism and well-being, modern Stoic Donald Robertson has developed the Stoic Attitude and Behavior Self-Assessment Scale, or SABSS. This scale is a test that anyone can do at home to determine how close their beliefs are too stoic attitudes.

The SABSS test consists of 20 statements about stoic beliefs and attitudes, followed by ten statements about stoic behaviors and life strategies. There is also a question to determine if the participants consider themselves practitioners of Stoics. The individual identifies as Stoic may or may not agree to uphold Stoic principles or use Stoic strategies.

Participants are asked to rate each statement on a scale of one to five, with five meaning "strongly agree" and one meaning "strongly disagree." This allows shadows of agreement and disagreement with Stoic principles. For example, you can give a rating of five to the claim that life's goal is happiness, but a rating of three to the claim that virtue is all that is needed for happiness.

The study of the SABSS questionnaire has produced some exciting results. As Stoicism predicts, prioritizing pleasure over virtue seems correlated with low levels of happiness and well-being. Stoic beliefs and attitudes were associated with higher levels of satisfaction. However, stoic life strategies and behaviors turned out to be more critical to well-being than stoic ideas.

The study is not enough to establish causality yet, but it seems that living like a Stoic will do more for your general well-being than merely thinking like a Stoic. Given a choice between stoic habits and stoic beliefs, you should focus on developing good habits and letting the views take care of themselves. Cognitive-behavioral therapy teaches us that thoughts, emotions, and actions are part of a feedback loop. By taking stoic-type steps, you can change your dreams, resulting in changes in your feelings.

Stoic habits

The SABSS study identified four specific stoic habits as the most important in promoting happiness and general well-being.

The first was "mindfulness," defined as paying close attention to your actions and the judgments you make in daily life. Instead of acting without thinking or making judgments without consideration, you should carefully weigh your thoughts and actions.

The second was to question his mental impressions before accepting them. Ancient Stoics compared this practice to a sentry who challenged anyone who approached the guard post. Do not allow any thought to enter the door; Be suspicious of your impressions.

The third was to think of yourself as part of the social whole rather than as an isolated individual. Marco Aurelio talks about this always in his Meditations, reminding himself that "what does not harm the hive does not harm the bee."

The fourth was negative visualization, numbing yourself to potentially disturbing experiences by imagining them in advance. This practice could be the original inspiration behind desensitization practices in cognitive behavioral therapy. Of course, it's essential to not only visualize whatever scares you but also imagine yourself handling it stoically. It wouldn't do you any good to visualize collapsing or plummeting into negative emotions!

These four practices are an excellent introduction to the stoic practice. Be aware of your actions and judgments, be suspicious of your impressions, think of yourself as part of a social whole, and imagine the worst before it happens. With such a simple set of daily goals, anyone can start practicing Stoicism right away.

In Stoic practice, the right actions performed for the wrong reason are merely appropriate, while correct activities performed for the right reason are called "perfect." Proper behavior is the first step toward happiness, and perfect practice is the culmination. The SABSS study suggests that appropriate action is enough to make significant improvements in your life, even if you are not yet capable of perfect behavior.

In practical terms, this means that a "person who progresses" can be significantly happier practicing Stoicism and that greater well-being and freedom are not restricted to the Sage.

While many more studies will have to be done before we can say anything definitive about the effects of stoic practice, there is certainly enough evidence to be optimistic. Rather than being an outdated and irrelevant philosophy from the distant past, Stoicism is beginning to be supported by the most up-to-date research in positive psychology.

Chapter 11: Everyday Stoicism

Now that you understand the basics of Stoicism and how stoics deal with everyday problems and emotional turmoil, you may be wondering how to start. The stoic idea is surprisingly simple, but progressing as stoic is not so simple. As with any skill, stoic thinking requires a lot of practice. These simple exercises are not necessary to prepare Stoicism, but they are likely to be useful in the early stages. Some of them may seem a bit harsh and puritanical the first time you read them, but they are based on the daily practical psychology of the Stoic school. By being strict with yourself in the early stages, it will be much easier for you to incorporate stoic resilience and self-discipline into your daily life.

Expand your affection: Let's say you have a favorite cup of coffee or a beloved old fishing rod or any other object that you particularly like. People often become emotionally attached to favorite objects like this. As a beginner in Stoicism, you are likely to be upset if you drop your favorite mug and break it, or if your beloved old fishing rod fell off the back of the boat and disappeared into the lake. Every time you pick up this precious item, ask yourself what it is, and answer honestly. It's just a coffee, and there are plenty of other suitable cups of coffee out there. It is just a fishing rod, and there are many good fishing rods. Instead of focusing on the specific object, try expanding your feeling of affection to include the broader category to which the object belongs. Epictetus suggests doing this even when he kisses his son good night or hugs his spouse, telling himself that he is merely kissing or hugging a human being. As with anything else in Stoicism, it's probably wiser to start small rather than take this advice to such an extreme environment.

These things happen: Sometimes, we understand things better from a small distance. Generally, we do not overreact to a situation unless it affects us personally because it is easier for us to see the case as it is. For example, if you were at a friend's house and your friend's son spilled a glass of milk, you certainly wouldn't be irritated by such a minor incident. What would you say? Probably "these things happen" or something like that because it is true that these things will happen. What happens when your child spills a glass of milk? If you are like many other parents, you are likely to be irritated by your child's carelessness and say something like, "I have asked you a thousand times to be more careful." Is there any real difference between the two situations? Exists, just the amount of distance between you and the source of stress. Practice saying to yourself, "these things happen," even in cases where you are directly involved. If you can make this a habit, you will begin to find that it is easier to look at your own life how you would see someone else's life, with enough distance to remember that "these things happen."

Do not speak: The phrase "loud but quiet" is a cliche and may remind you of a type of John Wayne character: Stoic on the outside, any emotional turmoil could be underneath. In the practice of Stoicism, "appropriate" actions are considered proper training for "perfect" activities, so being stoic on the outside can help you become stoic on the inside over time. Epictetus advises his students not to speak too much, saying only a few words and only when necessary. It doesn't go so far as to prohibit conversation, but it does tell your students to avoid any of the "common themes" that tend to make people emotionally excited. Most importantly, Epictetus says to avoid talking about other people and their actions. Don't praise them, don't blame them and don't compare them to each other. Why? Some activities are commendable, and others are not. Some actions deserve blame or shame. People can be easily compared to each other in several ways: this one is smarter, that one is stronger. Never mind. Blaming, praising, and comparing have the same problem. They divert their mind from their proper focus, which is always their actions and never anything external. According to Epictetus, his silence during inappropriate conversation can even stop him, preventing people from repeating harmful gossip and innuendo. Praise and compare have the same problem. They divert their mind from their proper focus, which is always their actions and never anything external.

Control your laughter: Epictetus says that he did not laugh too often and that he did not laugh too hard. This may seem a bit harsh, and Epictetus is probably the most stringent of all Stoics. However, it is not that there is something wrong with laughter. After all, joy is one of the "good feelings" that even a Sage can safely consent to. The reminder to control your laughter is a training exercise to keep your mind focused and self-disciplined as a stoic. Also, laughter is often cruel in some way. Imagine a coworker telling a funny story, the theme of which is the stupidity and incompetence of one of your other coworkers. Is it a story you can safely laugh about or a situation where you must remain silent? If you can control your laughter in that situation, you will also avoid criticizing others. Like the speech of a stoic,

Avoid vulgar language: It would probably take a sage not to swear in some circumstances, like hitting the thumb with a hammer. Epictetus knows this, but he still asks his students not to declare, if possible, and to keep it to a minimum, if they simply can't help but curse. Yelling something colorful when you hit your thumb with a hammer is more like an "impression," an unintended reaction rather than a choice. Swearing casually or excessively is more like "assent," the acceptance of false judgment. Like all the other exercises in this chapter, you should consider this more as a training exercise than an absolute rule. That said, it's hard to imagine stoic oath often or out loud.

Avoid vulgar entertainment: Again, it is not that any particular type of show is good or bad. In the Stoic view, the good and the bad are never found in external things, but only in your reaction to them. From rock shows to professional wrestling to horror movies, the things people do to pass the time are indifferent. However, popular forms of entertainment generally attempt to provoke intense emotions. The better the show, the more excitement it causes. It is usually best for a Stoic to avoid popular (and exceptionally vulgar) entertainment for training purposes. If you find yourself in such an event, you can still use it as an opportunity for stoic practice. First, try not to get caught up in the emotions around you. If everyone else screams and stomps, avoid doing the same. Second, avoid any show of superiority or condescension. Try to remain calm and unaffected, without appearing to disapprove of others. If you can avoid being swept away by the current of emotion, it will also be easier for you to do so in your daily life.
It should be noted that the Stoic philosopher Seneca wrote plays, including at least eight tragedies. A stoic should avoid any entertainment based on the crude manipulation of extreme emotion, but that does not mean that you cannot enjoy a good movie or a good book. It will also be easier for you to do this in your daily life. It should be noted that the Stoic philosopher Seneca wrote plays, including at least eight tragedies. A stoic should avoid any entertainment based on the crude manipulation of extreme emotion, but that does not mean that you cannot enjoy a good movie or a good book. It will also be easier for you to do this in your daily life. It should be noted that the Stoic philosopher Seneca wrote plays, including at least eight tragedies. A stoic should avoid any entertainment based on the crude

manipulation of extreme emotion, but that does not mean that you cannot enjoy a good movie or a good book.

Avoid luxury: To teach himself how to do without, Epictetus advises living a life of intentional minimalism. Don't buy the fanciest cut of meat or that bottle of expensive single malt Scotch whiskey. Don't wear designer clothes. Don't buy or build the most luxurious house. Epictetus says to limit yourself to what is merely useful, never beyond mere necessity. Seneca, much more luxurious, was not so hard. He only advocated living such a minimalist lifestyle for a few days of each month. Both approaches are training methods rather than absolute rules. Minimalism, like luxury and refinement, is something external. However, having necessities won't make you addicted to luxury, but living a lavish lifestyle will make it much harder for you to deal with difficulties if necessary.

Be careful with sex: Sexuality is such a powerful biological instinct that most people would find it difficult to abstain from sex altogether. If you are not in a long-term committed relationship, Epictetus says it is best to refrain if possible, but acknowledges that it will not be possible for everyone. If you don't think you can avoid it, it's best to be careful. Do not overdo it and do not participate in anything harmful or exploitative. While staying at the highest level, you can handle, avoid giving the impression that you look down on people who do things differently than you. Stoicism generally teaches us to be tough on ourselves but easy on others. Emphasizing their high level of behavior is contrary to endurance as not having a standard of conduct. This is a delicate line to walk since people who notice that you do things differently will often assume that you are looking down on them, even if you haven't given them any reason to think about it. While keeping your actions at a high level, try to project a calm and non-judgmental attitude on the effects of others. That way, you can avoid both extremes.

"May the best win": This saying exemplifies the stoic attitude toward athletic competition. The way Epictetus puts it is slightly different. He says you want the winner to be the one who ends up winning. Strictly speaking, the best man could lose due to chance, and a stoic still wouldn't bother about it because it would always be something beyond the control of the will. Still, "may the best man win" is close enough for our purposes and will prevent you from worrying too much about the outcome of a particular game. Many people get very excited about their favorite team, excited when their team wins, sad when they lose. Your team's record of wins and losses is not under your control, so, like anything else outside, you are indifferent to a Stoic. That does not mean that you cannot have a "preferred team" as a practicing stoic. Remember, indifferent things can still be preferred or not preferred. Even if you have a preferred team, your underlying attitude should be "let the best win." If you look at the game with that mindset, you won't be disappointed with the results, no matter what they are.

What would Epictetus do: Epictetus himself does not say "what Epictetus would do." It tells us to imagine what Socrates or Zeno would do, especially when he meets a famous person. It is hard to believe that the fearless Socrates or the noble-minded Zeno behave without dignity and self-esteem in front of someone alive, not even a powerful and dangerous ruler. To the modern Stoic, asking, "What would Epictetus do?" It is an equivalent exercise. If you have to meet with the CEO of the company or perhaps a politician, don't say anything you can't imagine Epictetus doing in the same situation. This exercise can help you avoid doing or saying anything you may regret later, no matter how nervous you feel about meeting the big man.

Don't tell too many war stories: Even if you have lived a life full of action and emotion, other people may not want to hear it as often as you think. The ups and downs of life can be entertaining, and the worst experiences are often the wildest anecdotes. At social events, like parties, people often tell stories about their adventures. For a stoic in training, the risk is that you focus too much on the opinions and reactions of your audience. Do you want them to laugh and think you're funny, to be surprised by your courage, or to envy your exciting experiences? In all of those situations, your mental focus is somewhat out of your control. Some of the most entertaining anecdotes involve bad decisions and their consequences. Are people laughing with you, or are they laughing at you? As with profanity and sex, Epictetus doesn't ban anecdotes entirely, but he says they don't tell stories about your adventures very often. Also, if someone else is telling a tale about something objectionable, they should make it clear, through their response, that they don't want to hear that kind of story.

Be a fatalist: The ancient Stoics were fatalists; they believed that the gods predestined much of life. To Marco Aurelio or Seneca, complaining too loudly about his life is like telling the gods that they made a mistake. It won't fix any problems you have, but it will tend to distance you from the gods. Of course, you don't have to believe that everything is predestined or worry about angering God to practice Stoicism. Even if the events are not predestined, you can accept what is out of your control. Still, thinking of games as decrees of Fate can be a useful exercise because it reduces the tendency to want things to be different when nothing can be done. Epictetus suggests using a line from the Greek playwright Euripides as a maxim:

"I happily follow him; and i didn't
Evil and miserable, I must follow him still.

When something cannot be changed, you have to live with it. If you cheerfully accept it, you won't feel bad about it. If you don't take it, you will have to go through it anyway, but it won't be perfect. As Euripides says, accepting fate without complaining is a sign of genuine wisdom.

Memento Mori: The Latin phrase memento mori means "to remember death." It is not intended to be gloomy, but a simple reminder that our time is limited. We all have to die, and none of us knows when our time will end. In one of her letters, Seneca talks about checking the time. Some people always want to see the time of day, but never think more about how much time they have left to live. If you knew you were exactly ten years older, how would you spend the remaining time? What if it was only ten more months or ten more hours or ten more minutes? If you weren't sure how much money you had left in your checking account, you would be wary of spending a single dollar for fear of an overdraft. According to Seneca,

Negative display: The phrase "negative visualization" probably sounds like the exact opposite of all the good-feeling and positive-thinking advice you've heard. As counterintuitive as it is, negative visualization is a fundamental technique of stoic daily practice. It is not intended to make you sad or anxious, but to vaccinate you against sadness and anxiety, like a mental vaccine. The basic idea behind negative visualization is simple.

Instead of telling yourself that bad things won't happen, you tell yourself that they will happen and handle it.

It's a good idea to start small, rather than tackle life's significant anxieties right away. Before doing anything, you should visualize the irritating things that usually happen. For example, if you go to the movies, you should imagine talking or a tall man sitting in front of you without taking his hat off. Remember that you don't just plan to go to the movies; You go to the film while keeping your mind calm and collected. If people end up talking during the movie or blocking their vision, it should be more natural not to get irritated because you prepared in advance.

Once you have some negative visualization experience, start applying it to things that are more serious than trivial irritations. For example, if you want to ask your boss to approve an important project, tell yourself that they will not agree to meet you. If she agrees to meet you, she will cancel or reschedule the meeting. If the meeting happens, she will ignore or disagree with everything you say. If she approves of the project, she will insist on changing her plans and managing the process. By imagining all the things that would generally stress you out in that kind of situation, you can avoid getting stressed when and if they happen. Paradoxically, this can even reduce the chances that any of these things will end up happening.

As an experienced practitioner of negative visualization, you should deliberately visualize the worst things that can happen. Illness, homelessness, injury, death — anything that scares you should be the subject of a harmful visualization exercise. By imagining frightening things in your mind's safety, you can reduce your fear reaction until it disappears, leaving you free from that particular anxiety.

Conclusion

In this book, you've learned about the history of Stoicism and the great Stoic thinkers whose ideas have survived to the present day. You've learned the basics of the Stoic practice, including the four passions to avoid and the three good feelings to cultivate. You've learned how to respond to first impressions with Stoic pragmatism and critical thinking, develop more resilience and self-discipline, and manage emotional turmoil with the Stoic mindset. You've learned how Stoicism has inspired some of history's most significant leaders, how it has influenced modern psychology, and how you can apply it in your daily life.

Thanks again for your support!

CPSIA information can be obtained
at www.ICGtesting.com
Printed in the USA
BVHW061215250521
608096BV00013B/2630